MY FIRST LOOK AT PETS

CATS ARE FUN, LOVABLE PETS

Cats

VALERIE BODDEN

CREATIVE EDUCATION

Published by Creative Education

123 South Broad Street, Mankato, Minnesota 56001

Creative Education is an imprint of The Creative Company

Designed by Rita Marshall

Photographs by Getty Images (Tony Evans / Timelapse Library, GK Hart / Vikki Hart,

Coneyl Jay, Dorling Kindersley, Kathi Lamm, Ryan / Beyer, Jeffrey Sylvester, Steve Taylor)

Copyright © 2007 Creative Education

International copyright reserved in all countries. No part of this book may be reproduced

in any form without written permission from the publisher.

Printed in the United States of America

Library of Congress Cataloging-in-Publication Data

Bodden, Valerie. Cats / by Valerie Bodden.

p. cm. — (My first look at pets)

Includes bibliographical references and index.

ISBN-13 : 978-1-58341-457-6

I. Cats—Juvenile literature. I. Title. II. Series.

SF445.7.B63 2005   636.8—dc22   2005050691

First edition 9 8 7 6 5 4 3 2 1

Cats

Cat Basics

Some people say that cats have nine lives. That is because cats are good at landing on their feet when they fall. They usually do not get hurt.

Almost all cats have long tails. Tails help cats balance. Cats have big eyes, long **whiskers**, and triangle-shaped ears. They have claws on the ends of their toes. They

CATS AND KITTENS USE THEIR CLAWS A LOT

can pull the claws into **sheaths** when they are not using them to scratch or climb.

Cats like to be active at night. They can see very well, even in the dark. Cats have a good sense of hearing, too. Cats can meow, hiss, and purr.

Most cats meow only at their owners. They do not usually meow at other cats.

Choosing a Cat

Cats make great pets. Some people choose to have kittens as pets. Kittens are usually playful. Other people like to have older cats as pets. Older cats can be easier to care for.

Cats come in lots of different colors. Some cats have black, white, gray, or orange fur. Other cats are more than one color. Their fur might have stripes or spots.

There are 66 million pet

cats in the United States.

They are the most common pets.

NEWBORN KITTENS LIKE TO PLAY AND EAT

Some cats have very long fur. Others have short fur. One kind of cat even has curly fur. A few cats have no fur at all!

Most cats weigh about as much as a human baby. Male cats are usually bigger than female cats.

THERE ARE LOTS OF DIFFERENT KINDS OF CATS

Cat Care

Cats do not need a special house or cage. Some cats like to sleep on a blanket or in a basket. Other cats like to sleep on their owner's bed!

Cats need a **litter box**. It should be cleaned often. They also need healthy cat food and lots of water. Cats should be brushed at least once a week. But most cats do not need baths.

CATS WILL SLEEP ALMOST ANYWHERE

Just like kids, cats need regular check-ups. A **veterinarian**, or vet, makes sure cats are healthy. The vet gives cats **shots** to keep them from getting sick. Most pet cats live 12 to 15 years.

Cat Fun

Cats like to be on their own more than some other pets. But they still like to spend some time with their owners.

Cats like to rest a lot.

Most cats sleep more

than 14 hours a day.

SOME CATS LIKE TO REST OUTSIDE IN THE SHADE

Sometimes cats like to be petted. They may want to be held, too. When holding a cat, you should put one hand under its chest. Use your other hand to carefully support its back legs.

Cats need some playtime every day. Cats like to play with lots of toys. Some like toy mice. Others like little balls. Many cats like to play in paper bags or boxes. All cats like to know they are loved!

KITTENS SPEND A LOT OF TIME PLAYING

Hands-on: Cat Mask

Have you ever wanted to be a cat? Give it a try by making a cat mask!

What You Need

A paper plate

Crayons

Eight pipe cleaners

Glue

Brown construction paper

Scissors

What You Do

1. Color the paper plate brown.
2. Draw two ears on the construction paper. Have a grown-up help you cut out the ears. Glue them to the top of the plate.
3. Have a grown-up help you cut eyeholes in the plate. Draw a cat nose and mouth below the eyes.
4. Glue four pipe cleaners on each side of the mouth to make whiskers.
5. Hold up your mask and practice your meow!

SOME CATS HAVE LONG FUR AND WHISKERS

Index

Words to Know

litter box—a special box that cats go to the bathroom in

sheaths—coverings that protect a cat's claws when they are not being used

shots—medicines that are given through needles

veterinarian—an animal doctor

whiskers—long hairs that grow near a cat's mouth and help it feel things

Read More

Blackaby, Susan. *A Cat for You: Caring for Your Cat.* Minneapolis: Picture Window Books, 2003.

Horton-Bussey, Claire. *101 Facts About Kittens.* Milwaukee, Wis.: Gareth Stevens, 2001.

Ring, Susan. *Caring for Your Cat.* Mankato, Minn.: Weigl Publishers, 2003

Explore the Web

Pet Care: Cats http://www.animaland.org/asp/petcare/catgames.asp

I-Love-Cats.com http://www.i-love-cats.com/catfunandgames.html

Enchanted Learning http://www.enchantedlearning.com/subjects/mammals/cats/cat/Catprintout.shtml